What's the Difference?

Plays About Tolerance

By Catherine Gourley

CRABTREE
Publishing Company
www.crabtreebooks.com

Crabtree Publishing Company

www.crabtreebooks.com

Project coordinator: Kathy Middleton
Editor: Reagan Miller
Proofreader: Molly Aloian
Production coordinator: Ken Wright
Prepress technicians: Ken Wright, Amy Salter

Written, developed, and produced by
RJF Publishing & A+ Media

Project management: Julio Abreu,
    Robert Famighetti
Managing editor: Mark Sachner
Associate editor: Anton Galang
Design: Westgraphix LLC / Tammy West
Illustrations: Spectrum Creative, Inc.

Library and Archives Canada Cataloguing in Publication

Gourley, Catherine, 1950-
    What's the difference? : plays about tolerance / Catherine
Gourley.

(Get into character)
ISBN 978-0-7787-7364-1 (bound).--ISBN 978-0-7787-7378-8 (pbk.)

    1. Toleration--Juvenile drama. 2. Children's plays,
American. I. Title. II. Series: Get into character

PS3557.O86T64 2010   j812'.54   C2009-906780-3

Library of Congress Cataloging-in-Publication Data

Gourley, Catherine, 1950-
 What's the difference? : plays about tolerance / by
Catherine Gourley.
    p. cm. -- (Get into character)
 ISBN 978-0-7787-7378-8 (pbk. : alk. paper) -- ISBN 978-0-
7787-7364-1 (reinforced library binding : alk. paper)
 1. Toleration--Juvenile drama. 2. Difference (Psychology)--
Juvenile drama. 3. Cultural pluralism--Juvenile drama.
4. Children's plays, American. I. Title. II. Series.

 PS3557.O915W43 2009
 812'.6--dc22
                                        2009047083

Crabtree Publishing Company

www.crabtreebooks.com   1-800-387-7650   Printed in the USA/122009/BG20091103

**Published in
Canada**
Crabtree Publishing
616 Welland Ave.
St. Catharines, ON
L2M 5V6

**Published in the
United States**
Crabtree Publishing
PMB 59051
350 Fifth Avenue, 59th Floor
New York, New York 10118

**Published in the
United Kingdom**
Crabtree Publishing
Maritime House
Basin Road North, Hove
BN41 1WR

**Published in
Australia**
Crabtree Publishing
386 Mt. Alexander Rd.
Ascot Vale (Melbourne)
VIC 3032

Series Consultants

Reading Consultant: Susan Nations, M.Ed.; Author/Literacy
Coach/Consultant in Literacy Development, Sarasota, Florida.

Content Consultant: Vinita Bhojwani-Patel, Ph.D.; Certified
School/Educational Psychologist, Northfield, Illinois.

Contents

Who's Got Game? 4

Think It Over 16

Breaking News 18

Think It Over 30

Your Turn 32

Glossary 32

About the Author 32

Note to the reader: Be sure to look at the Glossary on page 32 to find definitions of words that might be unfamiliar.

Who's Got Game?

Liz and Erika are a couple of seventh graders who meet at a summer basketball camp. They have hoop talents, but they also have big egos. Can two star ball players from diverse backgrounds learn to work together for a goal greater than their own athletic glory?

Characters:

Narrators 1, 2, 3

Liz Thomas, *a seventh grader who plays on a city-league basketball team*

Erika Hudson, *a seventh grader who plays on her middle-school team*

Talia, *a college student who works as a camp counselor*

Lena Walters, *a former professional basketball player*

Basketball coach

Scene 1

Narrator 1: On the campus of a large university, girls in the seventh and eighth grades from across the state have arrived for a week-long summer basketball camp.

Narrator 2: Many of the girls have come with friends from their schools' basketball teams. Liz Thomas, however, stands alone. Her school doesn't have a basketball team. She plays on a team in a city league.

Talia: *(approaching Liz)* Hi, are you Liz? I'm Talia. You're from my former school! They didn't have a team when I played there either. Like you, I played on a team in the city league. Then I went on to play in high school and college.

Liz: *(feeling relieved)* That's awesome! It's nice to meet you!

Talia: You look a little lost. The first couple of days at camp are always hard. Trust me, it gets easier. You'll have a great time, meet new friends, and learn a lot on the court, too! Come with me. I'll get you registered.

Narrator 3: Liz smiles, again feeling a bit relieved. Just then, the coach blows a whistle, silencing all the girls.

Coach: Listen up, ladies! We have a great week planned, but it's going to be hard work! Our special guest this week is a former pro—Lena Walters. We're going to make sure you don't get this confused with being on vacation!

Narrator 1: The girls groan and laugh. They are excited to be on a college campus and in the presence of a pro.

Coach: Ladies, you have one hour to settle in. Unpack. Meet your roommates. Break the ice. I want everyone back at ten sharp for drills. *(claps her hands)* Go, go, go!

Narrator 2: The excited girls hurry from the gymnasium. Liz turns quickly, almost knocking another girl over.

Erika: Ow! That's my foot you stepped on! Watch it.

Liz: I'm sorry. Are you okay?

Narrator 3: The girl doesn't answer. She hurries out the door to catch up with her friends.

Scene 2

Narrator 1: Liz finds her room in the dorm. Sitting on the bed is Erika, the girl whose foot she accidentally stepped on.

Erika: *(surprised and a bit disappointed)* You? You're my roommate? But I thought they'd pair me with someone from my school!

Liz: What school do you go to?

Erika: Kennedy Tech. What about you?

Liz: Midtown Middle.

Erika: So we're from the same town. How come we never played your school?

Liz: We don't have a school team.

Erika: Then why are you here?

Liz: *(defensively)* I play on a team in a city league, and I'm here for the same reason you are—to improve my game. What did you think?

Narrator 2: Erika shrugs. She begins to unpack her stuff—upscale sneakers, T-shirts, and shorts, all with designer labels.

Narrator 3: Liz opens her own duffel bag. Her clothes seem plain compared to the fancy wardrobe Erika is unpacking.

Erika: You any good at basketball?

Liz: Definitely. How about you?

Erika: *(boastful)* Just wait and see. See you on the court.

Liz: *(mutters to herself)* So much for breaking the ice.

Scene 3

Narrator 1: An hour later, the players run through drills while the coach, counselors, and Lena Walters take notes.

Narrator 2: The staff is deciding how to divide the girls into teams, based on both the positions they play and their ability.

Lena: Who's the girl who keeps losing control of the ball when she dribbles with her left hand?

Talia: That's Erika. She goes to a private school.

Lena: And that one, the one charging down the court?

Talia: That's Liz. She plays on a city league team. She and Erika are roommates. We paired them because they're from the same city but have different backgrounds.

Lena: That Liz is quick.

Coach: But careless. She needs discipline. She fouls a lot.

Narrator 3: They watch as each girl shoots from the outside. Both of their shots swish through the net.

Lena: Nice shots!

Scene 4

Narrator 1: After lunch, the girls rush to the gym. They can't wait to find out which teams the coach has put them on.

Erika: *(to one of her friends as she looks at the bulletin board)* Are you kidding me? It's bad enough I have to room with her. Now I have to play on the same team.

Narrator 2: Erika doesn't realize that Liz has overheard her. Later, Liz is talking with Talia.

Talia: So, how are you and your roommate getting along?

Liz: You mean the little rich girl? She's a "princess" with an attitude.

Talia: Give her a chance. You may learn some things from her. And you can teach her a few moves, too.

Narrator 3: That night in their room, Erika confronts Liz.

Erika: So you think I'm a princess?

Liz: Who told you that?

Erika: I have friends here, you know. They heard you talking to Talia. I don't like this setup any more than you do!

Liz: So why don't you ask them for a new roommate? Maybe they'll put you with your precious friends!

Narrator 1: Erika doesn't answer. She turns off the lamp above her bed. Both girls lie in their beds, their backs to one another.

Scene 5

Narrator 2: Throughout the week, the girls compete—each one trying to outdo the other. During the games, Erika does not pass the ball to Liz, even when Liz is open.

Narrator 3: Likewise, Liz refuses to set screens for Erika so she can get around the player guarding her and shoot.

Narrator 1: The one time Liz finally does set a screen, she gets called for a foul.

Coach: You see what's going on here? Each girl wants to outshine the other.

Lena: I can see that. It happened to me, first year of college.

Coach: I don't need two star players. I need team players. I don't think they know the difference.

Lena: Let me talk to them tonight privately and see what's up with them.

Narrator 2: That night, after lights out, Liz and Erika hear a knock on their door. They both sit up, a little startled at first.

Lena: Hey girls? You still awake? It's Lena!

Erika: Lena! What does she want?

Liz: I don't know.

Narrator 3: Liz opens the door. Lena smiles brightly. She has brought with her two baseball caps. They have the logo of Lena's pro basketball team on them.

Lena: I brought you these. Everyone will get one on Saturday at the awards ceremony, but I thought I'd give you yours early to give you a little inspiration on the court.

Erika: Wow, Lena. Thanks.

Liz: This is great. I love it.

Lena: So, do you two have a few minutes to talk?

Liz: Just us? Sure!

Lena: I've been watching you both. How come you guys aren't playing together on the same team?

I DON'T NEED TWO STAR PLAYERS. I NEED TEAM PLAYERS. I DON'T THINK THEY KNOW THE DIFFERENCE.

Erika: But we are on the same team.

Lena: You don't play that way.

Liz: Erika hogs the ball.

Erika: She never sets screens for me.

Lena: Women weren't always allowed to play the game, did you girls know that? People thought we were too frail, too weak.

Narrator 1: The girls look at each other. Both wonder where this private talk is going.

Lena: When they did allow women to play, they had special rules. Each team had nine players, not five. The court was divided into three sections, with three players from each team in each section, and each player had to stay in her own section. Players couldn't dribble more than three times before they had to pass. That's what society thought women were capable of—or rather *not* capable of. It wasn't ladylike to sweat!

Liz: I don't believe that!

Lena: It's true. For decades, the women's game was much different from the men's game. But that was a long time ago. Since then, countless female athletes proved society wrong. So when I see you two working against each other the way you do, it makes me sad.

Erika: Sad?

Lena: Yes. Instead of working against one another, you two need to work together so you can show everyone that you are capable of playing as a team.

Narrator 2: Lena gets up and goes to the door.

Lena: You've both got game. But you'll never make the pros—or even a college team—until you figure out a few things about yourselves.

Liz: Like what?

Lena: Like what you have in common, not how you are different.

YOU'VE BOTH GOT GAME. BUT YOU'LL NEVER MAKE THE PROS—OR EVEN A COLLEGE TEAM—UNTIL YOU FIGURE OUT A FEW THINGS ABOUT YOURSELVES.

Scene 6

Narrator 3: After Lena leaves, the two girls lie in the dark, thinking.

Erika: Do you think she gave that speech to everybody?

Liz: No.

Erika: I don't either. You know, my mother didn't want me to come here. She goes to my games and all, but she wants me to be a biologist like her. She thinks basketball is just a nice hobby.

Narrator 1: Liz sits up, turns on her light, and looks at Erika.

Liz: My mother expects me to babysit my younger brothers after school. Half the time I miss the games. When I tell her I want to play college ball, she just says it's a dream I should forget about.

Erika: So why can't you play ball in college?

Liz: Exactly!

Erika: Still, she let you come here. That means something.

Liz: I hadn't thought of it that way. So how did you convince your mom to let you come here?

Erika: I didn't. My dad did. He says I need to work on my ball-handling skills.

Liz: No offense, but he's right. You don't seem very confident with your crossover dribble. What's that about?

Erika: No *offense*, but why do you charge into people so you get called for fouls? My toes are still sore from the first day I met you!

Narrator 2: Liz begins to laugh. Then Erika starts laughing, too. The ice, at last, has broken.

Scene 7

Narrator 3: On the last day of camp, the coach and the counselors present special awards—including most improved defensive player and highest scorer.

...WHY DO YOU CHARGE INTO PEOPLE SO YOU GET CALLED FOR FOULS? MY TOES ARE STILL SORE FROM THE FIRST DAY I MET YOU!

Coach:	Our final award—and perhaps the most important of all—is for sportsmanship.
Lena:	I'm happy to present this trophy to Erika and Liz.
Erika:	*(jokingly, to Liz)* We have to share a trophy, too?
Narrator 1:	Everyone laughs. But Lena surprises them with two separate trophies.
Narrator 2:	Before they leave camp, the girls say their goodbyes. It's only been one week, but they have bonded in a way that neither of them had expected.
Liz:	When we get to high school, we'll be on opposite teams. Then we'll have to play each other.
Erika:	Better watch out for me, Lizzie! I know all your moves!
Liz:	Girl, I only showed you the ones I wanted you to see!
Narrator 3:	Both of the girls laugh, lightly bump fists, and look forward to continuing their competition—and their friendship—in the years to come.

The End

Think It Over

1. Compare and contrast Liz and Erika. How are the two girls different? What do they share in common?

2. Erika is disappointed that she isn't rooming with a friend from her own school. But how does having Liz as a roommate help Erika become a better team player?

3. Liz arrives at camp not knowing anyone. How might this affect her behavior?

4. What exactly does Liz mean when she calls Erika a "princess with an attitude"? Is she right to say such a thing about Erika? Explain why you do or do not think so.

5. How does Lena get the girls to look beyond their own interests and learn to play together as a team?

Breaking News

When a confrontation between teens in a small town leads
to an ugly act of vandalism, the media—and the law—step in.
Is the defacing of a business owned by a Hispanic man who
recently moved to town a "harmless" teenage prank or an
act of intimidation? How should the victims face
those responsible for issuing hurtful ethnic slurs?

Characters:

Narrators 1, 2, 3

Roberto, *a teenager visiting his
Uncle Antonio during the summer*

Antonio Álvarez, *owner of a used car dealership*

Tim Townsend, *a popular radio talk show host*

Johnny, *a car mechanic*

Chuck, Dan, *local teenagers*

News reporters 1, 2

Police officer

Colleen Callahan, *owner of a supermarket in town*

Jules Bergman, *owner of a local deli*

Scene 1

Narrator 1: Antonio Álvarez recently moved from the city to a small town to open a used car dealership. Last week, his 14-year-old nephew came to visit for the summer.

Narrator 2: Roberto helps out at the dealership by answering the telephone in his uncle's office.

Roberto: *(answering telephone)* Álvarez Autoworld. How may I help you? *(pauses)* Sure, please hold. I'll get him. *(hands phone to Antonio)* It's someone from the paper.

News reporter 1: Mr. Álvarez, I wonder if, as a new resident of this town, you have any reaction to the comments made by Tim Townsend on his radio talk show yesterday.

Narrator 3: Antonio hesitates. Although he does not listen to Townsend's talk show, his mechanic Johnny does. Antonio knows that Townsend's comments are often intended to trigger heated debates from his listeners.

Antonio: No. I prefer not to comment on anything Tim Townsend says. Thank you. *(He hangs up.)*

Narrator 1: Johnny shakes his head at Antonio.

Johnny: I wish they had asked me! I'd have given them a piece of *my* mind. Yesterday he called all Hispanics "lazy border jumpers."

Roberto: What does that mean—border jumpers?

Johnny: You know, that's how he refers to illegal immigrants. He had his callers all worked up. He said Hispanics are taking good jobs from hard-working Americans.

Antonio: I know he is insulting, but you should just turn him off. Why do you keep listening to his show?

Johnny: Because a wise man knows who his enemies are.

Antonio: They are not the enemy, Johnny. This Tim Townsend knows nothing about us and doesn't care, either. What he does know is that some people are fearful of anything or anyone new. So he gets them all riled up.

Johnny: You don't get it, Antonio. They don't want us here.

Roberto: *(interrupting)* Who are "they"?

Johnny: *(to Roberto)* "They" are certain people in this town who have a problem with anyone who isn't just like them. You know, maybe I'll just call that guy myself.

Narrator 2: He reaches for the phone, but Antonio stops him.

Antonio: Don't you understand? He's baiting you. It's a talk show. Unless people get worked up enough to call in and sound off, he has no show. Without a show, there are no advertisers. Without advertisers—

Roberto: There is no radio station, right?

Antonio: There are better ways to deal with this than getting pulled into a shouting match.

Narrator 3: Antonio picks up the telephone and dials the station.

Roberto: What are you going to do?

Antonio: Just listen.... *(into the telephone)* I'd like to speak with the station's advertising manager, please.

Narrator 1: After a moment, Antonio explains to someone else his displeasure with Tim Townsend's name-calling.

Antonio: Until he apologizes, I will no longer advertise on your station. That is correct. Starting now. *(He hangs up.)*

Johnny: We are just one small business, Antonio. How can that make a difference?

Antonio: It may not. But I've done what I think is right. Remember, you guys—no one can make you feel bad about yourself unless you let them. Don't let them get under your skin.

Scene 2

Narrator 2: A few days later, Roberto brings the morning paper to his uncle. On an inside page is a story about the station and its popular talk show host, Tim Townsend.

Roberto: It worked!

Antonio: *(reading aloud from the article)* "Mr. Townsend regrets comments he made on his talk show about members of the Hispanic community. The statements made by Townsend do not reflect the attitude of the radio station or its management."

UNTIL HE APOLOGIZES, I WILL NO LONGER ADVERTISE ON YOUR STATION. THAT IS CORRECT. STARTING NOW.
Álvarez
Antonio Álvarez

Johnny: (*surprised*) Apparently you weren't the only one to pull your ads. It says that Callahan's Supermarket also stopped advertising—and Bergman's Deli, too.

Roberto: (*turning on the radio*) Let's hear what he says today!

Narrator 3: Soon, Tim Townsend's voice echoes from the radio.

Tim Townsend: I never meant to offend anyone in particular, especially not the Hispanic citizens of our town.

Johnny: Okay, so he apologized. I still don't think it's enough.

Scene 3

Narrator 1: A few nights later, a community organization holds a carnival to raise funds for the fire department.

Narrator 2: At the carnival, Roberto wanders away from Johnny, who is talking with some friends. As Roberto waits in line at the Ferris wheel, Johnny waves and calls out to him in Spanish. Roberto answers, also in Spanish.

Narrator 3: Suddenly, two boys push ahead of Roberto.

Chuck: (*to Roberto*) What do you think you're doing?

Roberto: Waiting to ride the Ferris wheel.

Chuck: Who said you could ride the Ferris wheel?

Roberto: Anybody can ride it, I guess. It's a free country.

Dan: Yeah, well it's not your country. Why don't you go back to where you came from, border jumper?

Narrator 1: Roberto clenches his fists. It is the same slur the talk show host used on his radio program.

Roberto: This *is* my country!

Chuck: Then why don't you speak English?

Roberto: What's your problem?

Dan: Our problem is you and people like you, border jumper. You don't belong here.

Narrator 2: Once Roberto is on the ride, the boys taunt him. He is sitting ahead of them. When the ride ends, they follow him through the carnival, taunting him.

Narrator 3: Roberto is younger than Dan and Chuck. He searches the crowd for Johnny, knowing he'd be safe with him.

Narrator 1: But Roberto is alone and scared. He runs across a field toward his uncle's dealership. Chuck and Dan chase him.

Narrator 2: As Roberto nears the dealership, he sees a light on in the garage. He opens the door.

Johnny: Hey! Back so soon? Weren't you having a good time?

Roberto: Uh . . . sure, but I didn't know where you went.

Johnny: I had to finish up some work on this transmission. What's going on? Is anything wrong?

Narrator 3: Roberto looks outside. Chuck and Dan are gone.

Scene 4

Narrator 1: The next morning, Antonio discovers ethnic slurs painted on the side of his building. Someone has broken the windows on many of the cars. The sides of eight cars are also painted with the words *border jumper* and *go home*!

Johnny: I told you that talk show guy was trouble.

Antonio: Tim Townsend didn't do this!

Johnny: No, but his listeners probably did!

Narrator 2: Antonio calls the police. As they arrive, so do reporters. The vandalism incident is a breaking local news story.

Narrator 3: The excitement draws a crowd to the dealership. Roberto sees Dan and Chuck with their bicycles across the street, watching the police and reporters. Roberto is sure they are the ones who vandalized Antonio's dealership.

Police officer: *(to Antonio)* Do you have any reason to suspect someone is trying to intimidate you?

Antonio: No, no reason at all. Everyone here has been very friendly to me ever since I moved to town.

Police officer: *(to Roberto)* What about you?

Roberto: *(softly)* I don't know anybody here except my family.

Antonio: My nephew is visiting for the summer.

Narrator 1: The police officer studies a damaged car. Then she bends over to pick something up from the ground. It is the ticket stub from a carnival ride.

Police officer: Hmm.... Looks like somebody stopped by here after the carnival to cause some trouble. *(She looks at Roberto, who is biting his lips.)* Do you know anything about this? Were you at the carnival?

Narrator 2: Roberto is torn between speaking up and keeping silent. If he speaks up, he'll be snitching, and that might mean even more trouble for his uncle.

Narrator 3: If he does not speak up, the boys who taunted him may get away with what they did.

Roberto: *(hesitating)* Uh...yes. I was at the carnival, and some boys followed me here.

Johnny: So that's why you came back so early!

Antonio: If you know who they are, Roberto, you must tell.

Narrator 1: Roberto looks across the street. Chuck and Dan are still there, watching him.

Roberto: *(He points to the boys.)* They called me a border jumper and chased me back here.

Narrator 2: Dan and Chuck jump on their bikes and race away.

Roberto: *(to Antonio)* I tried to walk away. I tried not to let them get me all worked up, like you said. But they wouldn't let up and ended up chasing me.

Antonio: You did the right thing, Roberto.

Scene 5

Narrator 3: The next day, Roberto, Antonio, and Johnny are watching the news on TV.

News reporter 2: *(to TV audience)* After being identified, two teenage boys have admitted they vandalized the Álvarez car dealership. They have apologized. Charges are pending.

Johnny: I don't buy their apology. Is that the message here? It's okay to insult people as long as you apologize?

Roberto: *(to his uncle)* What will happen to them?

I DON'T BUY THEIR APOLOGY. IS THAT THE MESSAGE HERE? IT'S OKAY TO INSULT PEOPLE AS LONG AS YOU APOLOGIZE?
Alvarez Autoworld
Go Home

Antonio:	This kind of vandalism is pretty serious. The judge might put them in a juvenile detention center.
News reporter 2:	*(to TV audience)* I have with me now the owners of Callahan's Supermarket and Bergman's Deli. What do you think of this vandalism in your town?
Colleen Callahan:	This is a good place to live and raise a family. We are not going to tolerate hate crimes of any kind.
Jules Bergman:	That's right. It doesn't matter who the victim is. When one group is targeted, we all pay the price.
News reporter 2:	*(to audience)* As you can see, some residents are pulling together to support the Álvarez family. Police say the boys will appear in juvenile court this week.
Antonio:	What a waste! Putting such young boys in a detention center doesn't solve the problem. It just hides it.
Johnny:	Not putting them away allows the problem to grow!
Roberto:	Maybe Uncle Antonio's right. What good will it do for these guys to go to a detention center? Maybe someone should try organizing things to bring kids together.
Antonio:	Hmm. Not a bad idea, Roberto.

Scene 6

Narrator 1:	The next morning, Tim Townsend stops by the dealership.
Tim Townsend:	Mr. Álvarez, I think what I said may have had something to do with all this. Some of the words those kids painted were the same ones I used on my show, and I want you to know that I really do regret what I said.
Antonio:	I appreciate your saying that. By the way, I want you to meet my nephew, Roberto. Those kids harassed him before they came over here. He had an idea you might like to hear. Go ahead. Tell him, Roberto.
Roberto:	I just thought it might be good to try organizing things for kids to do—you know, to help keep them out of trouble, maybe even help them see we're all not so different. There are programs like this where I live. I can find out a little about how it works, but you'll have to find someone who can help get it going here.

I JUST THOUGHT IT MIGHT BE GOOD TO TRY ORGANIZING THINGS FOR KIDS TO DO—YOU KNOW, TO HELP KEEP THEM OUT OF TROUBLE, MAYBE EVEN HELP THEM SEE WE'RE ALL NOT SO DIFFERENT.

Tim Townsend:	Sounds like a good thing. Let me know what you come up with, and I'll see what I can do to help, okay?
Roberto:	*(a little surprised)* Sure. I'll let you know.
Antonio:	Good. Now, what can we do for those boys?
Roberto:	Well, since I'm the guy they picked on, maybe I should talk to the judge or someone.
Antonio:	I'd be willing to drop the charges if they agreed to some kind of community service.
Tim Townsend:	Well, my words might have gotten them riled up. I understand they've never done anything like this before. I'd like to think that coming up with something they can do to keep their records clean would be a good solution to this for everyone.
Antonio:	Fine. Roberto and I will speak to someone, and if we need your help, we'll let you know.
Narrator 2:	Tim and Antonio shake hands, hoping that the community can move forward.

The End

Think It Over

1. Johnny and Antonio do not agree on how best to handle ethnic intimidation. What position does each take on this troubling issue?

2. Does Antonio's plan to withdraw his advertising from the radio station work? Provide a reason for your answer.

3. Did Roberto do the right thing by running away from Dan and Chuck? Provide a reason for your answer.

4. Why do reporters cover the story of the talk show host's apology and the vandalism at the dealership? Why is this considered news?

5. Tim Townsend apologizes to Antonio and says he is responsible. But is he to blame for the ethnic slurs painted on Antonio's building? Explain why you do or do not think so.

6. How might Roberto's idea for creating a program to bring kids together help fight intolerance? What other ways can you think of to educate people about diversity? Explain what these might be.

TIM AND ANTONIO SHAKE HANDS, HOPING
THAT THE COMMUNITY CAN MOVE FORWARD.

Your Turn

1. Research and write a few paragraphs describing the history of women's basketball. When did women first begin to play? How has the sport changed for women since its early days?

2. "Breaking News" ends without the reader knowing the fate of Chuck and Dan, although Antonio says he is willing to drop the charges and Roberto is willing to speak to the judge. Write a final scene set in the courtroom in which the judge passes sentence. Be sure the judge explains the sentence to the boys in a way that expresses your opinion about what kind of sentence they should receive, and why.

Glossary

dealership A business that buys and sells things, usually cars

dorm (short for *dormitory*) A building or area where people sleep

ethnic slurs Insults based on a person's race or culture

harass To annoy or intimidate, causing trouble for someone else

immigrant A newcomer to a country

intimidation Pressure or threats

registered Signed up or recorded as a participant

screen A move in basketball in which a player legally blocks an opposing player's view or path so a teammate can drive in and make a shot

transmission The part of a motor vehicle that transmits power from the engine to the wheels

vandalism Deliberate destruction of property

taunt To provoke or challenge someone with insulting comments

About the Author

Catherine Gourley is the author of the award-winning nonfiction series *Women's Images and Issues of the 20th Century: How Popular Culture Portrayed Women in the 20th Century.* She is the national director of Letters About Literature, a reading promotion program of the Center for the Book in the Library of Congress.